piano

ACKNOWLEDGEMENTS
Special thanks to: Lynne Austin-Dutton, Liz Walsh
& family, James Austin, Norma Dutton, Bernard
Dutton, Levine Andrade, Pete Riley, Andy Staples,
Chris Harvey & Iain MacGregor at SMT.

Voice over performed by Lynne Austin-Dutton.

Printed in the United Kingdom by
MPG Books Ltd, Bodmin

Published by SMT, an imprint of
Sanctuary Publishing Limited
Sanctuary House
45–53 Sinclair Road
London W14 0NS
United Kingdom

www.sanctuarypublishing.com

Picture Credits: Rex Features,
and Redferns
Design and Editorial: Essential Works

ISBN: 1-84492-040-2

piano

John Dutton

smt

CONTENTS

INTRODUCTION

When you pick up a book, you usually decide if it's for you within the first few seconds. So, let's get a couple of things straight. While this book is about helping you to play, and learning new things, we're into the same thing – making music and having fun! Making music doesn't have to mean years of study – some of the greatest music ever is very simple.

If we can get one thing across in this book, it's that the main factor in making music is you. Only you can make the music you play mean something. Without a human element, music is boring – and you'd turn that off straight away, wouldn't you? Music should be fun, exciting and good to listen to.

If you want to be a cool player, you're also going to have to touch on a few important technical areas. Don't be afraid to take things one step at a time – trying to rush through can get frustrating. When you start to feel improvements, though, you'll be hooked.

And, the more you know, the more you can do and the more fun you'll have. By the end of the book, you may have surprised yourself...

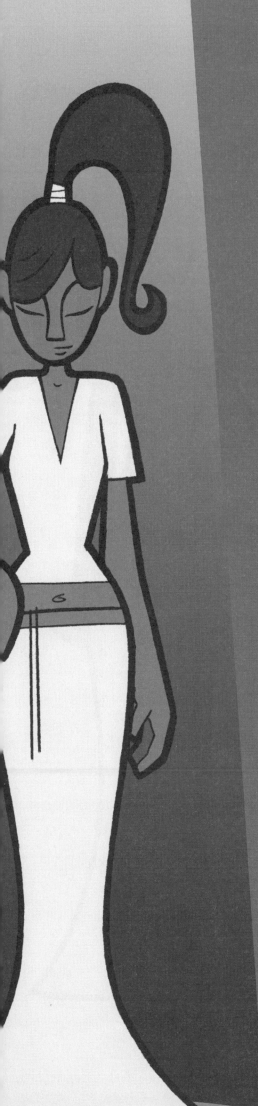

MEET YOUR TUTOR

Your guide to the extraordinary world of piano playing is Keys. Keys will help guide you through the book, giving you advice and help along the way. She'll find answers to problems that often come up and will help in her own unique way.

She certainly is one cool piano player, so let's make her acquaintance…

KEYS IS HERE TO GUIDE YOU…

'Hey dudes! I'm Keys, and I'm here to help guide you through this book. I gotta say, there's a lot of great stuff in here, but don't try to take it on board all at once. Take your time and you'll get your playing on the right track!'

ADVISE YOU…

'Why do I love the piano? Well, you can just sit down and play it, with other musicians or just on your own, if you feel like it. You can create so many colours and moods with the piano — it is the best instrument in the world!'

TEST YOU…

'Part of my job is to make sure you understand what's going on, so, at the end of each lesson there'll be a few questions on what you've just learned. Don't be fazed out — if you've learned things properly, you'll have no problem. On the other hand, if you've rushed through and you're cheating on me, I'll know straight away…'

HELP YOU ENJOY YOUR MUSIC…

'Music is fun, and like a never-ending journey — there's always more there if you want to find it! Remember, all great music comes from your soul.'

YOUR PIANO

One of the great things about a piano is that you can just sit down and play it. It doesn't need to be turned on or warmed up. The inner workings are usually hidden away behind a case and the only thing it needs to keep it sounding good is a tune-up every few months or so. Pretty amazing.

There are two types of piano – an upright and a grand. An upright is smaller than a grand piano, and is shaped differently. You'd be more likely to see a grand in a concert hall or large recording studio, where space isn't so tight.

Grand pianos usually cost a bit more than uprights, too. They both work on the same idea, though. At the heart of a piano is a wooden soundboard fixed to a big iron frame, to which metal strings are tightly wound. When you press down a key, a hammer strikes the string, making a sound. The wooden soundboard then amplifies the sound of the string being struck, giving the piano its unique tone.

To save space, an upright's strings run up from the bottom of the piano frame to the top. Lift up the lid and have a look at the way the hammer strikes the string when you press down a note. If you're lucky enough to have a grand piano, you'll see that the strings are longer and run from front to back. This horizontal arrangement of the strings is what gives a grand piano its distinctive shape.

If your piano is an upright, it will have two pedals – the 'sustain' pedal on the right, and the 'soft' pedal on the left. The sustain pedal in particular needs to be used carefully, but you'll see how good it makes you sound later on…

Does the piano look like a big complicated instrument to you? Well, it's not really – like most things in music there is a pattern. Look down at the keyboard and cast your eyes from the bottom (left) to the top (right). You'll see there is a succession of white notes, followed by a succession of black notes, then white notes, then black notes, and so on.

You'll probably have guessed that because these same patterns of black and white notes continue across the whole keyboard they must share some kind of relationship. You'd be correct. While there are 88 notes on a full length piano keyboard, there are actually only 12 different ones (including the black notes) which just get repeated in a pattern across the keyboard:

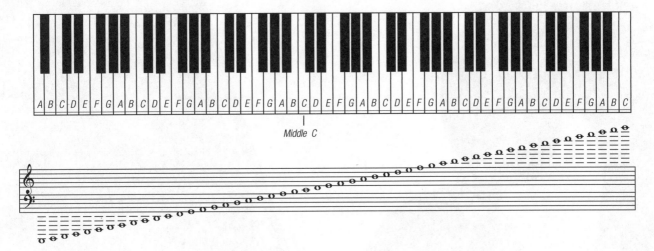

Middle C

The arrangement of black and white notes can help you remember which letter names belong to which note. Look at a C and there are two black notes above it, like a pair of candles. Look at an F and there are three black notes above, like a fork. It may sound a bit loopy, but thinking of a pair of candles for C and a fork for F is an easy way to remember the basic layout of notes.

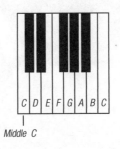

Middle C

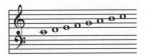

To help you know which fingers to use, we're going to refer to each finger with a number from 1–5. In both the left and right hands, 1 is the thumb and 5 is the little finger, with the other fingers numbers – 2, 3, 4 – in-between.

READING MUSIC

If you're going to become a serious player, you need to see what music looks like written down. Don't think of this as a downer – without doing it, you can't make sense of all the things I want to show you. We'll do it in stages, and – I promise you – it's nowhere near as hard as you may think!

You've probably had a look at written music before – maybe when you flicked through this book. Music is written on what we call a stave, or staff – a series of five lines that look like this:

As we play the piano with two hands, there are two staves joined together on a piece of piano music – the top one for the right hand and the bottom one for the left.

The right hand staff will usually have a symbol like this 𝄞 at the start of each line. This is known as the treble clef.

The left hand will usually have a symbol like this 𝄢. This is known as the bass clef.

As a result, a typical piano part would be laid out like this:

Whenever we go through something, I'll show you what it looks like written down, starting in the next lesson.

So, now that we've got some basics out of the way, let's get down to business…

LESSONS

SITTING AT THE PIANO

When you sit down to play, the chances are that you'll naturally sit around the middle area of the keyboard. This makes sense, as you then have roughly equal areas to play with your left and right hands. It also means that you're sitting near a note known as 'middle C', the C note found in the middle of the keyboard, between the two pedals.

YOUR GOALS

GOAL 1
To sit comfortably at the piano. It's no good expecting to play if you're not comfortable, and bad habits die hard... so get this right early on!

GOAL 2
To play a simple exercise with both hands.

GOAL 3
To see what music looks like written down.

THEORY

What we're aiming for is to sit in a natural position. We all slouch around when watching TV or crashing out at home, but if you get into habits like that when playing piano, you're soon going to get backache!

IN PRACTICE

STEP 1

Sit on a stool (or a chair without arms) that has a really good, solid seat. If it sags in the middle, it's no good – it must be firm. Don't sit right back on the seat – sit towards the front end of the seat to help your weight rest on your bottom.

STEP 2

It may feel a bit strange, but try and sit up so that your back is as straight as possible. Making sure you sit right on your bottom helps a lot.

STEP 3

Try and find a seat at a height that allows your forearms to angle down slightly towards the keyboard. It doesn't matter if this means you can't reach the pedals yet.

EXERCISE

PART 1: THE RIGHT HAND

1. You're now in good shape to start playing. The next thing is to find middle C again, and play a short series of notes to get acquainted.

2. Put your right hand on the keyboard, with your thumb on middle C and your other fingers resting on the white notes that follow (D, E, F and G).

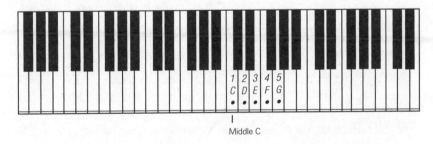

Middle C

3. Lift your thumb up and press down on middle C – use the CD to check you have the right note. When the note has sounded, bring up the thumb and depress the next note, D, using your second finger. When D has sounded, bring up your second finger and depress E with your third finger. Carry on until you reach G, using your little finger, and play the notes back down to middle C.

PART 2: THE LEFT HAND

1. We're going to do the same thing with your left hand, but we're going to start on the C below middle C. This distance between two notes that share the same letter name is called an 'octave'.

2. So, put your left hand on the keyboard, with your little finger on the C an octave below middle C. As you did with the right hand, rest your other fingers on the adjacent white notes going up the keyboard (which are D, E, F and G).

Play the exercise the same way as you did with the right hand, up to the G (this time played with your thumb) and back down again to the C.

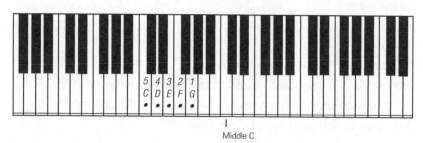

Middle C

PART 3: LOOKING AT A WRITTEN PART

The next step is to see what this looks like written down. Let's see what middle C looks like, taking the treble clef first:

...and the bass clef...

The right hand exercise you've played in this lesson looks like this:

The left hand exercise looks like this, with middle C written in as a reference:

PROBLEM?

Anything that's new can feel strange at first. Just making sure you're sitting properly can seem to be a bit of a pain, but it's something that you'll appreciate the more you play. Likewise, it can take a while to feel comfortable with playing something different, such as the exercise in this lesson. Don't worry if you seem to be taking time to learn things – suddenly you'll find things come together and start to connect. When that happens, it's a great feeling, and it'll get you hungry for more…!

PART 4: PUTTING BOTH HANDS TOGETHER

The final task in this lesson – as no doubt you've guessed already – is to play both hands together. There's no need to play the exercise quickly, in fact the slower you do it the better.

TIP

Sometimes when you try something new, it's easy to get into a habit of holding your breath. So, once you've sat down, before you play, try putting your shoulders up to your ears. Then say, out loud, 'one, two, three, four', and relax your shoulders back down. You should find this helps a lot…

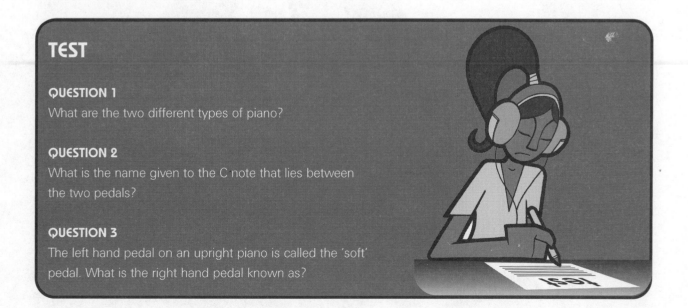

TEST

QUESTION 1

What are the two different types of piano?

QUESTION 2

What is the name given to the C note that lies between the two pedals?

QUESTION 3

The left hand pedal on an upright piano is called the 'soft' pedal. What is the right hand pedal known as?

GETTING THE BASICS SOUNDING GOOD

When you played the exercise in the last lesson, how did it sound to you? Was it like the one on the CD? To get things sounding smooth and even, I'm going to show you how to get your basic technique on the right track. Get into this now and you'll make quicker progress later!

YOUR GOALS

GOAL 1
To understand about good tone and to start getting things smoother and more even.

GOAL 2
To learn a more advanced exercise, based around a major scale.

GOAL 3
To look at a larger range of notes on the right- and left-hand staves.

THEORY

When you listen to top piano players, they seem to make everything they play sound great, even easy things. You can, too. One of their secrets is having a good tone, which is the quality of sound that you get out of the piano. We're going to run through a couple of crucial issues that will get you on the right track.

IN PRACTICE

PART 1: REACHING THE BOTTOM OF EACH NOTE

STEP 1

We'll try this out one hand at a time. Going back to the Lesson 1 exercise, put your right or left hand on the keyboard, with your fingers just resting on the notes, not playing them. When your fingers are just resting on the notes like this, you shouldn't be all tensed up – it just wastes energy. Remember that playing piano requires a lot less effort than you may think.

STEP 2

Keeping the same basic posture as before, play the exercise again, as slowly as you like. Keep the wrist as stable and relaxed as you can – don't get into a lot of unnecessary arm movement.

STEP 3

Try and only use your fingers to play the notes – don't move your body around unnecessarily. Keep the ends bent and try to get each finger to reach the bottom of its note – not skating on the top.

Making sure you reach the bottom of each note doesn't mean you have to play loudly. Just play at what seems like a normal volume. After a little while, you should notice your sound getting a bit more even, and this will help you get more 'feel' for the way the keyboard plays.

PART 2: PLAYING LEGATO

The next thing is to make sure we're joining up the notes as much as possible. This is called legato playing.

Legato is an Italian term meaning 'smoothly'. Used in the right place, legato playing can help put a lot of polish onto your sound. To show you what it does, we'll use the Lesson 1 exercise again.

STEP 1

Use your right hand on its own and play the first note with your thumb. This time, before you bring up the thumb to release the note, lift up your second finger.

STEP 2

At the same time the second finger goes down, bring up the thumb. The idea is that the change from one note to the next is as smooth as possible. Try not to allow the notes to overlap each other (listen to the CD to hear what I mean).

STEP 3

Carry on and do the same thing with your other fingers. When you've got it comfortable with your right and left hands separately, play both hands together.

If you're doing both the things we've gone through in this lesson – playing legato and making sure you reach the bottom of each note – you should hear a noticeable difference from when you first played the exercise in Lesson 1.

EXERCISES

Before we can move on and start playing, we need to develop this concept a bit. At the moment, we're just playing from middle C to G, using all five fingers in sequence. We're going to carry on playing up the keyboard a bit more, until we reach the C an octave above middle C.

PROBLEM?

You'll have noticed that some of your fingers are stronger than others. To help even things out more, a good tip is to play them in different (alternating) rhythms. Listen to the CD to give you a guide.

TIP

Some people think that being good is all about how fast you can play. Even if it means missing a few bits out, or never quite getting it right. But it's not! Think of all the tunes and songs you really like, and, nine times out of ten, they'll be musically very simple, and often surprisingly easy to play. So, if you want to make quick progress, concentrate first on getting the foundations right, and making the basic things sound good. Otherwise, you'll get found out later, believe me…!

PART 1: THE RIGHT HAND

1. Using your right hand on its own first of all, play the first three notes – C, D and E, as before.

2. When you get to the F, we need to change our fingering a bit. If you tuck your thumb underneath, you will have enough fingers left to play up to C.

C major scale, right hand

3. To get back down to middle C, just retrace your steps back to the F. Once you've played the F with your thumb, put your third (middle) finger over to the E.

4. You're now back to your original hand position, and the last two notes, D and middle C, can be played with your second finger and thumb.

PART 2: THE LEFT HAND

1. Because you start with your little finger, you can keep the hand in the same position until you reach the G, with your thumb.

2. To play the next note, A, just put your third (middle) finger over the top; you can then play the B with your second finger and C with your thumb.

3. To go back down just play it in reverse, like you did with the right hand a moment ago.

C major scale, left hand

What you've just done is to play a C major scale. There are two types of scale we'll look at in this book, major and minor. Scales are like the nuts and bolts of music – they may only be exercises, but are still really crucial things to get a handle on.

C major is a good one to start with because it only uses white notes, and so is easy to remember.

TEST

QUESTION 1
What does the term 'legato' mean?

QUESTION 2
What is the name of the scale you have just learned?

BASIC CHORDS AND KEY SIGNATURES

Now that you know what a C major scale is, it's time to show you how you use certain notes in the scale to form a chord.

YOUR GOALS

GOAL 1
To understand what major chords are and play them using both hands.

GOAL 2
To explore new key signatures, using our ears to guide us.

PART 1: BASIC CHORDS

THEORY

When you listen to music, it isn't just made up of single notes, is it? Instead, most music is based around chords, which are groups of three or more notes played together. There is no limit to how many notes a chord can have, other than being able to play them all at the same time!

There are two types of scales, and chords, that you need to know, which are major and minor. They're very similar, apart from a few important differences. Because we've just done a major scale, we'll look at a major chord first.

A major chord takes three different notes from the major scale, the first, third and fifth, and plays them together – a C major chord, then, is made up from a C (the first note), an E (the third note) and the G (fifth note). Listen to how it sounds on the CD and then play these notes together yourself.

EXERCISE

1. To play this chord with your right hand, use your thumb on C, your third finger on E, and your little finger on G.

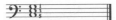

2. For your left hand, use your little finger on C, your third finger on E, and your thumb on G.

3. When you feel comfortable playing each hand on its own, try them both together:

And, that's all a basic C major chord is. Simple, eh? See how getting a grip on your scales can be really helpful in more ways than one.

You use chords all the time in music. As we move on, you'll see there are different types of chords, and different ways of playing them. Once you know the basic types of chords, you'll start to hear how they give music moods and character.

TIP

Remember what I said about piano playing needing less effort than you might think? Before playing a chord, find the notes first and rest the fingers you're going to use onto them. Don't just plonk your hand down. Lift your wrist and forearm slightly and bring them down to play the chord in a controlled way. Again, try and reach the bottom of each note.

PART 2: OTHER KEY SIGNATURES

If you want to play a piece of music, you can't just stick on C major. Next, we'll look at some more key signatures. I want you to understand just a bit about the way a major scale is made up, so there's a little bit of theory here – but remember, don't be afraid. There's nothing to it really!

THEORY

You will have noticed when you played C major scale that there were only seven different notes – C, D, E, F, G, A and B. Most scales only use certain notes from within an octave.

You can see that some of the notes are right next to each other, some are not. The gap between two notes that sit right next to each other is called a semitone. Notes that have a two-semitone gap between them are called a tone apart. The gap between any two notes is known as an interval.

C major is the only major key that only uses white notes. Every other major key has at least one black note in it. We call these black notes accidentals. Accidentals can appear in exercises such as scales, or in pieces of music.

Accidentals are known either as 'sharps' (written ♯) or 'flats' (written ♭). The number of sharps or flats in a scale make up its key signature.

IN PRACTICE

Major (and minor) scales are made up from a set order of semitone and tone intervals. Look at the diagram below and check out the order of a major scale.

The gaps between the notes are:

Tone (C–D)
Tone (D–E)
Semitone (E–F)
Tone (F–G)
Tone (G–A)
Tone (A–B)
Semitone (B–C)

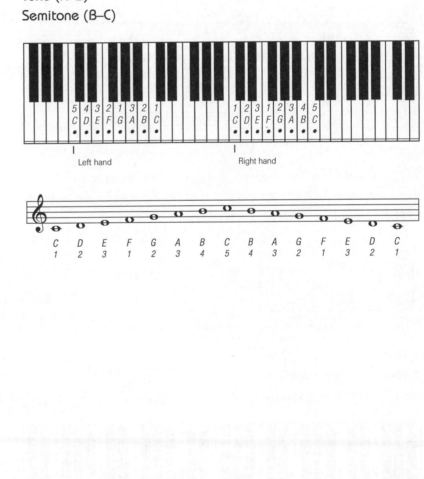

EXERCISE

Let's use this pattern of intervals to get to know some more major scales and chords. Each one has the same fingering as C major, so there's no need to panic! First up: G major. G major has one sharp, F sharp, in its key signature.

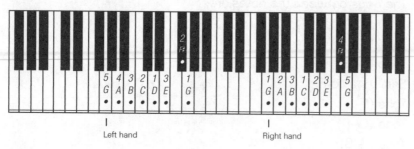

CD TRACK 9

G major scale, right hand

The key signature (in this case F sharp) is normally just written in at the front of the stave. To help remind you, I've also put it in front of the notes as well.

G major scale, left hand

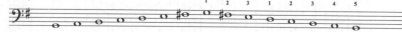

1. To play a G major chord, we do exactly the same thing as with C major. We take the first, third and fifth notes of the major scale (in the case of G major, G, B and D) and play them together.

Again, I've put the sharp signs next to the note on the stave, as well as the key signature at the start. A real piano part would just have the key signature at the start of each stave.

2. Next is D major, which has two sharps. We keep the F sharp we've already come across in G major, and add a C sharp:

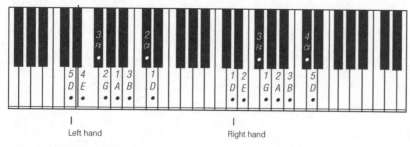

CD TRACK 10

D major scale, right hand

D major scale, left hand

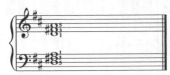

3. D major chord:

4. Next is A major, which has three sharps, F, C and G:

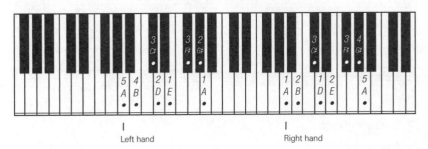

Left hand   Right hand

A major scale, right hand

A major scale, left hand

5. A major chord:

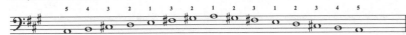

6. To finish this lesson, E major, which has four sharps, F, C, G and D:

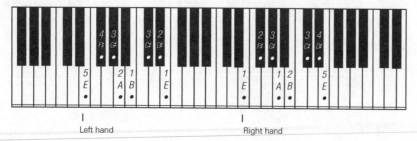

|
Left hand

|
Right hand

E major scale, right hand

E major scale, left hand

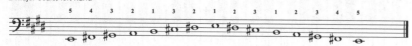

7. E major chord:

PROBLEM?

Have you experienced lifting something that feels a bit awkward or is too heavy? To try and manage it, you sometimes contort your body to help. If you're having trouble playing certain bits of a scale (and it's usually with the weaker fourth or fifth fingers), try and keep your hand position as normal. Don't be tempted to try and move your body around to 'help' play something. Just work at it slowly and it will come in time.

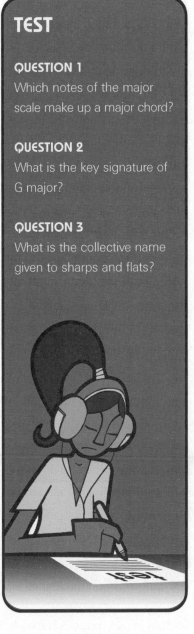

TEST

QUESTION 1
Which notes of the major scale make up a major chord?

QUESTION 2
What is the key signature of G major?

QUESTION 3
What is the collective name given to sharps and flats?

GETTING TO KNOW ABOUT RHYTHM

All this stuff about technique, and so on, is all very well, but I bet you're dying to play something. Well, we're going to start putting what you've learned into practice by looking at one of the main things that makes up music – rhythm!

YOUR GOALS

GOAL 1
To get to know about rhythm, basic notes and rests.

GOAL 2
To play a short piece with both hands.

PART 1: NOTE VALUES

THEORY

Music is made up from two main parts: harmony and rhythm. It's no use knowing about loads of scales and chords if you've got no rhythm – one can't work without the other!

Rhythm in pop music is based around a beat, or pulse. A good example of a beat is the solid bass drum part thumping away on a typical dance record (the CD gives an example). This gives you an idea of how rhythm runs through a track.

Now, over the length of a pop song there may be hundreds of beats, so the music is arranged into sections of either two, three or four beats at a time. These sections are known as 'bars'. Bars are separated from each other by 'barlines'.

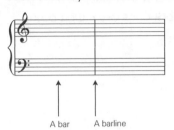

A bar   A barline

A lot of pop music (and everything in this book) has four beats to the bar. The amount of beats a bar has makes up its 'time signature'. Four beats in the bar is also known as 'common time', which appears on a stave like this:

This is the sign for common time (four beats in a bar)

CD TRACK 13

IN PRACTICE

STEP 1

So, let's put this into practice. Say we wanted to play a middle C along with the pulse, like that dance track bass drum was doing, it would look like this:

STEP 2

As you can see, a note written like this ♩ lasts for a beat and is known as a 'quarter note'. There are a few other note values that we'll use in the book. I'll put each of them in a bar of four, just the same as above.

LONGER NOTES

A 'half note' lasts for two beats.

A 'whole note' lasts for four beats, or the entire bar.

SHORTER NOTES

An eighth note lasts half a beat. One eighth note on its own looks like this ♪. When there are two or more in sequence, they are written down joined together. In a bar of four, there are eight eighth notes in a bar.

A sixteenth note lasts for a quarter of a beat, so there are sixteen in a bar of four.

As with an eighth note, two or more sixteenth notes in sequence are written down joined together. On its own, a sixteenth note looks like this ♬ .

PROBLEM?

When notes and rests have different length values, it can seem hard to read. If you get confused, counting out loud while playing really helps. Try to always keep feeling the beat, or pulse, running through the piece of music.

EXERCISE

Most music is made up of a combination of the different length notes. We'll try out a few short pieces, using each hand separately, to get you in the groove.

1. First of all, let's try these two pieces, one for each hand, which are just made up from quarter notes.

2. Now we'll do something similar, but bring in some eighth notes as well.

In this exercise, you need to put your thumb under here…

… and your second finger over, here. Try not to turn your wrist over too much, make your finger move instead. It will come in time!

3. And to finish off, a version that uses both hands together. The right hand plays chords, while the left adds in single lower notes to pin it down. This is a straightforward little exercise, but a lot of pop songs are made up with similar type parts.

PART 2: RESTS

THEORY

Think of a well-known song you like by your favourite band or artist.
When you sing along with it, there are gaps between notes, or between
phrases. Sometimes these gaps are tiny, and you can hardly hear them.
Other times they will last for a few beats, or even a few bars. The gaps
are called rests, and are crucial to giving music life and space.

IN PRACTICE

When you play a piano part, it will usually be made up of notes and
rests. All of the note values you've come across already have a rest of
the same length. It's pretty easy to see how they fit in.

Sixteenth note rest: ⅞
Eighth note rest: ૪
Quarter note rest: ૐ
Half note rest: ▬
Whole note rest: ▬

So, when you see a rest, it's simple – don't play for however long
the value of that rest is!

EXERCISES

1. Here are versions of Part 1, Exercise 1 with some quarter note rests:

2. …and Part 1, Exercise 2 with some quarter and eighth note rests:

3. To finish off, a version of Part 1, Exercise 3 with half note rests:

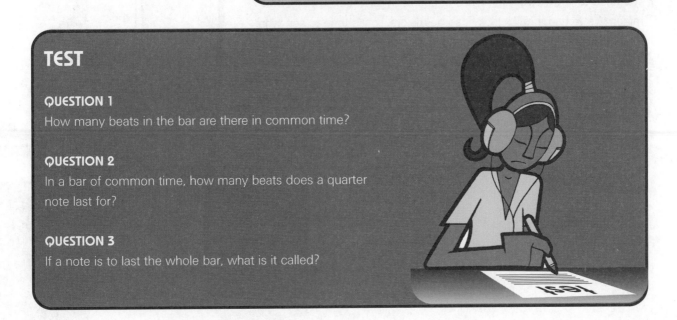

TIP

Remember that the purpose of this practice is to help get you playing some cool stuff by the end of the book. Don't worry if you have to look back at this lesson to remind yourself.

TEST

QUESTION 1
How many beats in the bar are there in common time?

QUESTION 2
In a bar of common time, how many beats does a quarter note last for?

QUESTION 3
If a note is to last the whole bar, what is it called?

MAJOR AND MINOR KEYS

Hey there! You're starting to get a grip on all this stuff now. One of the things about playing piano is that you can do so much, so read on and expand your mind!

YOUR GOALS

GOAL 1
To play, and hear the difference, between major and minor harmony.

GOAL 2
To learn a quick guide to sharps and flats.

GOAL 3
To play these in a cool-sounding exercise.

MINOR CHORDS – A QUICK RUNDOWN

You need to know two main types of chords in this book – major and minor. We've had a quick look at some majors, so it's time to see what minor chords are all about…

THEORY

Think of majors and minors as cousins – very similar, but with one difference: the third note of the scale is one semitone lower in the minor.

IN PRACTICE

STEP 1

The best way to understand this difference is for you to hear them against each other, so let's take a major chord first, let's say, D:

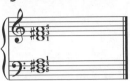

STEP 2

To make this into a D minor, we take the third note of the scale – F sharp (the middle note of the chord) – and put it down a semitone, in this case to a regular F:

EXERCISE

1. Play the major, then the minor, and you'll hear their different characters: a major chord has a happy, bright sound, and a minor chord has a darker, sadder sound. It's hard to believe that changing one note – the third note of the scale – makes the chord sound so different. But it does, with any major and minor chord.

MINOR SCALES

Just as a minor chord is very similar to a major chord, minor scales are very similar to major scales. All scales, whether major or minor, are made up from a set order of intervals, just a slightly different order. While we're definitely not going to wade through loads of theory here, look at the minor scales in the back of the book and learn as many as you can. If you want to know more about music theory, then it's a good idea to get a book that deals with it in more detail than we can here.

A LITTLE WORD ABOUT SHARPS AND FLATS...

As we go through the book, it will mean coming across 'accidentals'. You come across accidentals in the key signature and in front of a note on the stave.

There are two types of accidentals – sharps and flats. It's time to explain just a little more…

If you see a sharp sign next to a note, it means play that note a semitone higher:

If you see a flat sign next to a note, it means play that note a semitone lower:

Sometimes, the key signature is written in at the start of the stave, like this example of G major:

If you were playing a piece with this G major key signature, which has one sharp, F sharp, you would play every F in the piece as a sharp. It would not have to be marked separately with a ♯ sign.

TIP
When listening to major and minor chords on their own, it's quite easy to hear the difference between them. It can be harder in a piece of music. Try and notice how their character can change slightly, depending on how they are used. Again, try and reach the bottom of each note.

PROBLEM?

If you're playing a piece and it just doesn't sound right, remember to look at the key signature!

So, here are all the major chords we've learned so far, with their minor cousins:

TRACK 19 CD

TRACK 20 CD

TEST

We'll have an audio test in this lesson. On the CD I'll play all of these major and minor chords above, but in a random order:

QUESTION 1
Are they major or minor?

QUESTION 2
Can you find which actual chord it is on your piano keyboard?

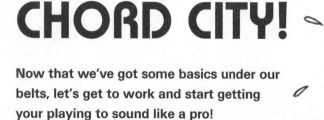

CHORD CITY!

Now that we've got some basics under our belts, let's get to work and start getting your playing to sound like a pro!

PART 1: ROOT CHORDS

THEORY

All the chords you've done so far have been in a basic form, what we call 'root position'. If you have any chord, for example C, and C (the keynote) is at the bottom of the chord, then it's in root position. Because they sound very solid and definite, root chords are usually used at the start and end of a track.

But we don't play every chord in root position – it would sound too straight. To hear what I mean, check out these root position chords, played one after the other:

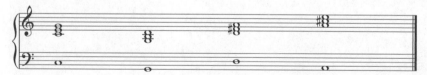

To give more variety of sound, we can use a mixture of root position and 'inversions'. Inverted chords use the same notes as root position chords, but just arranged in a different order. Full inversions would include the left hand, but, in this book, we'll only deal with the more basic forms of inversions, in the right hand only.

YOUR GOALS

GOAL 1
To play inversions of all the chords you've come across so far.

GOAL 2
To learn about seventh chords and playing a 12-bar blues.

IN PRACTICE

Look at C major root position, it uses C, E and G.

STEP 1

C major first inversion uses exactly the same notes, but has E at the bottom, with G and C above it:

STEP 2

A C major second inversion has G at the bottom, with C and E above it:

STEP 3

Using inversions means you don't have to move around the keyboard as much to play different chords, and stops the music from sounding boring. Let's play those four chords we did a moment ago, with a couple in root position and a couple inverted:

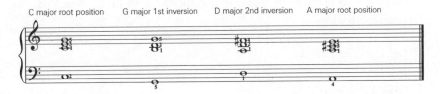

Sounds a lot smoother, doesn't it? In the pieces at the end of the book, you'll come across plenty of inversions of both major and minor chords. Remember that all of them just rearrange the notes that you'll find in a root position chord.

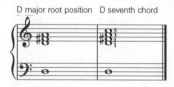

PART 2: BLUES CHORDS

When you play the piano, some notes sound nice when played together, and some of them clash and sound a bit nasty. The notes in normal major and minor chords all harmonise with each other well and sound pleasant.

But as we get into different types of music, like jazz and blues, chords are sometimes made up from notes that sound 'nice' together, with one or two 'clashy' notes mixed in.

When these nice and clashy notes make up a chord, they can blend together and, instead of clashing, have a definite character.

IN PRACTICE

Let's look at a couple of examples, starting with blues.

STEP 1

The crucial character of blues is extremely soulful. Normal major and minor chords, however good they sound, need something extra to put this soulful feeling across. So, blues playing uses a lot of seventh chords.

Straight seventh chords use a major chord as its base, like this D major example:

STEP 2

To make a D seventh chord (known as D7), we add a flattened seventh note. The seventh note of D major is C♯, so flatten it (which means take it down a semitone) to a normal C.

D major root position   D seventh chord

STEP 3

If you play just the bottom note, D, and the top note, C, together, they don't sound very good. But, when they're played as part of this D seventh chord, it blends in and gives it a definite flavour.

PROBLEM?

If you find it difficult to remember the sequence of chords in a 12-bar blues, don't worry, just try and let things happen. A 12-bar is one of the most comfortable-feeling patterns of chords in music. Don't get hung up, just get in there!

EXERCISE

A well-known format in blues playing is called a 12-bar. A series of chords is played over a 12-bar length, which is repeated over and over until the end. A 12-bar is very simple and popular for jamming over. You may well recognise the pattern. Let's have a blues jam in D!

A. Play the key chord (D) for four bars.
B. Play the fourth chord of the scale (G) for two bars.
C. Play the key chord (D) for two bars.
D. Play the fifth chord of the scale (A) for one bar.
E. Play the fourth chord of the scale (G) for one bar.
F. Play the key chord (D) for two bars.

1.

TRACK 23

2.

TRACK 24

BETTER, FASTER, SMOOTHER!

Just like an athlete has to train to improve and keep themself fit, a musician – whatever he or she plays – has to always try and improve their technique. A good technique allows you to play more styles of music, and play them better!

So, we're going to go through a few things that will help you play the tracks coming up at the end of the book. All the exercises are now arranged around four beats in a bar to get you used to note values.

PART 1: PLAYING ARPEGGIOS

IN PRACTICE

STEP 1

With a chord, like this C major, you play all of the notes together. In an 'arpeggio', you just play the notes separately, from bottom to top and back down again, like a scale:

You can use this fingering for all the right hand root position arpeggios coming up!

right hand

You can use this fingering for all the left hand root position arpeggios that follow!

left hand

Arpeggios are really useful because lots of piano parts are based around them. So, as well as improving your technique, you're helping yourself for later on.

YOUR GOALS

GOAL 1
To improve your finger strength and dexterity.

GOAL 2
To learn a few more topics on the way!

GOAL 3
To learn how to practise.

EXERCISE

1. So try out these arpeggios:

2. As before, the slower you do them, the better! When you feel comfortable with each hand separately, try putting them together. You should find this a bit easier than with scales, as the hand position stays the same.

Right hand… using root position and inverted chords:

3. Left hand… using root position and inverted arpeggios:

C major

You can use the fingering from the last left hand exercise for this one too!

C minor

You can use the fingering from the previous left hand exercise.

G major

You can use the same left hand fingering here as well…

G minor

Same left hand fingering here…

D major

Same left hand fingering here…

D minor

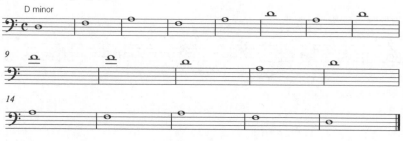

PROBLEM?

Sometimes you just can't get going. You feel like you're wasting your time. Every player knows these feelings, even the very best. Just remember – even though you may feel like you're not getting any better, every time you sit down and learn, you are. All of a sudden you can make a big leap forward, so don't give up!

TIP

Remember to do the things we talked about in earlier lessons – reach the bottom of each note, keep a good posture and don't get all tensed up. Another good tip, which I gave you guys earlier, is to do scales and arpeggios in different rhythms. It really helps to even your playing out. Listen to the CD for a guide.

PART 2: PRACTISING

OK… just about the most boring section of the book, right? I mean, who wants to sit there for hours on end, repeating a load of exercises?

Well, no one does, and that's why I've included a short section on it. You see, people often have the wrong idea about practising. The thing you should ask yourself, is, why are you even learning the piano? The answer is… because you love music!

Instead of taking about practising, we'll talk about learning. You learn all the time, even when you're not aware of it. When you listen to something on the radio, or a CD, you're actually taking things in all the time. The more music you listen to, the more ideas you'll have in your own playing.

So, there are two forms of learning – listening and working on your instrument.

IN PRACTICE

With listening, don't only put on tracks you like to hear. All cool players learn from every style of music. Open your mind to styles you might not have thought of, and listen to what the whole band is doing, as well as the piano.

Working on your instrument means doing something regularly, and if you want to make quick progress, every day. The main thing is, guys, work smart.

TEST

There's enough here to keep you busy, so no test in this lesson!

STEP 1

Do some basic exercises for a few minutes before you play anything else. Scales and arpeggios are good, but don't overdo them. Play them slowly and concentrate on getting a good tone.

STEP 2

If you're trying to learn a piece, break it down, don't try and do it all the way through. Look at the bits you're having most trouble with and get them comfortable. Don't ever just rush through it – you'll never get it right.

STEP 3

Try and do half an hour a day. That might seem like a lot, but you'll soon feel progress.

PUTTING THINGS TOGETHER

YOUR GOALS

GOAL 1
To use both hands together effectively.

GOAL 2
To know how, and when, to use the sustain pedal.

PART 1: USING THE LEFT HAND

It can be easy sometimes to think your left hand's not got as much to do as your right. Playing piano is definitely a two-handed business, though. While the left hand often plays a different type of part to the right, it's equally important!

The left hand does two main things: it usually plays the lowest part of whatever chord you're playing and gives the harmony a good solid foundation, and it helps keep the rhythm flowing.

EXERCISE

1. So, let's have a go! First of all, we'll take a bar of music in C major, where both hands play at the same time as each other:

2. This is all fine, but it's a little bit straight, isn't it? There's no groove. To help it along a bit better, we're going to change the left-hand rhythm ever so slightly.

Instead of playing four quarter notes in a row, we're first of all going to put a rest in place of the second quarter note. Just get used to the feeling of playing your right hand on its own on the second beat:

3. Next, we're going to put in another note, but this time an eighth note. It's got to be played on its own, in-between the second and third beats. Look at the music and you can see the order of the notes:

4. Now that sounds a bit more groovy, doesn't it? When you play that eighth note, try and make it a little bit quieter than the others, so it leads into that third beat.

You can change this slightly so the eighth note comes a bit later:

5. Another type of part the left hand can often play is like an arpeggio. This again helps keep the rhythm going, and gives a good foundation to the harmony:

PART TWO: USING THE RIGHT HAND

It's true that you'll play more chords with your right hand than your left. You'll also play more tunes, and solos, as well.

EXERCISE

1. There are lots of different bits that can make up a right hand part. There's the straight quarter note on each beat, in the style of the last example:

repeat

2. … you can easily groove this up a bit by making it all into eighth notes:

repeat

3. … and you could add the type of left hand part we used a moment ago:

repeat

4. … and you could mix it all up a bit, with quarter and eighth notes in the right hand:

repeat

5. … and finally try going round two chords, with a slight change in left-hand note values:

repeat

6. You'll come across these types of parts in the featured artist section later on. Why don't you try making up a few chords of your own?

PART 3: USING THE SUSTAIN PEDAL

The sustain pedal is one of the main things that can help you sound great. It's also possible to use it wrongly and make your playing sound messy. Believe me, there's nothing worse than that!

You probably have tried out the sustain pedal already, just to hear what it does. If you haven't, hold the pedal down and play a few notes, any will do. As long as you hold the pedal down, you can take your hands off the keyboard and the notes will still sound.

IN PRACTICE

You can't use the pedal all the time, because different chords can clash against each other and sound horrible. So, you use the pedal in two situations: to make the change from one chord to another as smooth as possible, and to keep sounding part of a chord while you play other notes.

STEP 1

Let's see how it works using a simple example.

No matter how good your legato playing is, the chord change in each bar is very hard to get sounding smooth. Enter the sustain pedal.

lesson 8   51

EXERCISE

You can keep the pedal held down over the same chord, then, as you play the first chord, depress the sustain pedal and hold it down for the whole bar. Then, I want you to try doing something that may feel a little strange at first.

Are you ready?

1. When you get to the end of the first bar, keep the pedal held down and take your hands off the keyboard. The first chord will still be sounding.

2. Find where your fingers go for the second chord, but don't play it – just rest your fingers on the keys.

3. Play the second chord and, at the same time, bring up the pedal. If you've done it right, the change will sound smooth. Depress the pedal again to help you onto the next chord.

4. Music is sometimes marked to show you where to use the pedal. It usually appears next to a pedal marking, as a line like this:

These markings show when you should start and stop using the pedal

When the line stops, take your foot off the pedal. But watch the music carefully, because you might have to use it again for the very next chord!

PROBLEM?

It can take a little work to get this feeling right, but you'll get it OK, I promise. Just concentrate on bringing up the pedal as you play the next chord, not before, not after. In this example, you'll want to use the pedal in each bar, so, when you've brought up the pedal, depress it again to hold down the next chord.

TIP

Where there are no pedal markings, only hold down the pedal over the same chord. When it changes, you can think about using it like we've done here. If you're in doubt as to whether to use the pedal or not, see what it sounds like without it first of all.

TEST

QUESTION 1

What is one of two main things that you would use the sustain pedal for?

QUESTION 2

As well as usually playing the lowest note of a chord, what does the left hand also do?

GETTING THE MOST OUT OF MUSIC

Why do you play music? Because you enjoy it.

Why do you listen to music? Because you enjoy it.

So, when you create music and give enjoyment to other people, that's quite special. But, what do people enjoy most about music?

The answer is... the way it makes them feel.

The most important element in your playing is not how good the instrument is, or how many exercises you know. Instead, the most important thing is you. Whether you think about it or not, your personality and soul comes out when you play. Even if it's something very simple.

So, what does this mean? Well, a few different topics, but all based around the same thing – putting human feeling into your playing.

YOUR GOAL

To learn about phrasing and dynamics.

PART 1: PHRASING

THEORY

If I asked you to read out a couple of pages of a book out loud, you wouldn't be able to say it all in one breath, would you? You'd have to stop now and again to get enough air.

So, when you play a piece of music, think about that, because just like you, music needs to breathe. This is part of a very straightforward, but absolutely crucial, issue – phrasing.

EXERCISE

Now, the kind of phrasing you use depends on the type of part you're going to play, so let's look at a couple of easy examples to get you into the groove.

1. This piano part is pretty simple – just a sequence of four chords. Play it through and see what you think.

2. Look at it again. Over the four-bar length, it feels as if it's in two sections – the first two bars and the last two bars. So, we'll put a little breath in-between to make this clearer. It looks like this:

We use this line over the top of the music to tell us where to take a breath. This means that you leave a tiny gap, so tiny you can hardly hear it. But play it with, and then without, the phrasing and hear the difference.

3. Here's a very simple right hand tune, first of all without any phrasing:

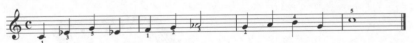

4. Now, follow the phrasing and let the music breathe:

TIP

When you have a written part, it'll usually give you phrasing marks to follow. If you're playing along in a band, maybe jamming or reading a chord chart, always think about phrasing. Every few bars (or sometimes much less), the music will rise and fall, and it will need a breath. Even if the other people you're playing with don't take much notice, make sure you do – you'll be a much better musician as a result!

PART 2: DYNAMICS

THEORY

So, we've got the music to breathe. But it still lacks something, doesn't it? Think about your spoken sentence again. You don't say every word at the same volume, do you? Instead you make more of certain words (if you're excited about something) and less of others (perhaps if you're whispering, or a bit sad). Remember what I said about the most important thing in making music being you? Well, this is where you let your inner self come out, and put a bit of soul into the music. To do this, we need to have a good balance of loud and soft. One is no good without the other!

IN PRACTICE

CD TRACK 32

STEP 1

Just as with phrasing, in a written part (like the ones in this book) there'll often be indications as to how to play. So that you know what these indications mean, we'll have a quick look at them now:

- f (forte) – loudly
- p (piano) – quietly
- mf (mezzo-forte)– fairly loudly
- mp (mezzo-piano) – fairly quietly
- crescendo (often marked cresc) – get louder
- diminuendo (often marked dim) – get quieter

PROBLEM?

It can be tricky at first to gradually play louder or quieter. Sometimes it happens a bit too quickly, or doesn't happen at all! When you practise, try playing four or five chords, starting loudly and getting softer, then the other way round. When you're playing a piece of music, look ahead and see how many bars you have to make the change.

EXERCISE

1. Have a look at this part, which includes some of these markings:

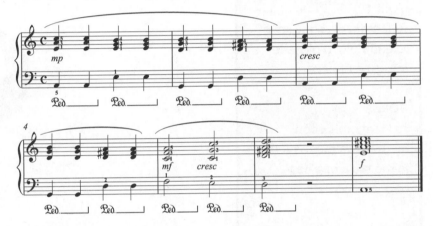

It starts at mf – fairly loudly, and gets quieter until, at the end, it's marked p (quietly). This fits in with the slightly sad feeling of the last (minor) chord.

Take notice of the phrasing, too.

2. Now, try something a bit more up-tempo:
This starts quietly and gets louder until at the end it's at f (loudly).

These are both simple examples, but you'll need to know these dynamic markings to play the tracks at the end of the book.

TIP

We've given you a lightning-quick guide to these subjects here, but enough to have made you think a bit. A lot of players don't make as much of dynamics and phrasing as they could, and they're poorer off for it. To be a serious player, you've got to keep an audience interested in what you're doing. So, make the music mean something. Make it yours!

TEST

QUESTION 1
What would the marking be for playing loudly?

QUESTION 2
What would the marking be for playing softly?

QUESTION 3
If the music is to get gradually quieter, how would it be marked?

QUESTION 4
If the music is to get gradually louder, how would it be marked?

PLAYING IN DIFFERENT STYLES

All good players are versatile. This means that they can have a good go at anything – rock, blues, jazz, pop – you name it. We need to see how some of the things we've covered work together in different styles.

YOUR GOALS

GOAL 1
To learn a bit about the role the piano plays in the style of pop.

GOAL 2
To learn a bit about the role the piano plays in the style of blues/ boogie woogie.

GOAL 3
To learn a bit about the role the piano plays in the style of jazz.

PART 1: POP

THEORY

The piano has been used for centuries as a backing instrument for songs. When modern pop music emerged in the '60s, bands like The Beatles used a piano behind some of their biggest hits, such as 'Hey Jude' and 'The Long And Winding Road'.

In the '70s, a new breed of pop piano players came along who wrote, and sang, their own songs. These included people like Elton John and Billy Joel. Today, Coldplay's frontman, Chris Martin, uses a piano at the centre of the band's sound.

IN PRACTICE

STEP 1

The piano might have a big part to play in pop music, but it usually has to work with the song. This often means the piano part is simple, but very effective!

STEP 2

The left hand usually has a particularly simple part, as there is a separate bass player in the band. If the left hand is playing too much, it can clash with what the bass player is doing.

STEP 3

When the right hand has a series of steady chords, try putting a slight accent on beats '2' and '4', along with the main snare drum beat.

PART 2: BLUES/BOOGIE WOOGIE

THEORY

One of the best known modern boogie woogie players is Jools Holland. However, Jools himself was influenced by old-school players, such as Jerry Lee Lewis and Albert Ammons. The overall style hasn't changed much – it's often based around a 12-bar chord sequence and uses a lot of straight seventh chords.

Part of blues harmony (and jazz, too) is the way 'clashing' notes are put with 'normal' chords like majors and minors. Even the top and bottom notes of a straight seventh chord will clash a bit if played on their own. When you add more notes to make up a chord, though, they stop clashing and make up part of the blues sound.

TIP

Remember that you're now playing with other people, as part of a band. Listen to what's going on around you as much as possible. Be confident, but try and make your sound fit in with what the band are doing. Keep it cool and keep it simple!

IN PRACTICE

STEP 1

Boogie woogie really chugs along. The left hand is usually at the centre of the rhythm and chord structure, while the right hand plays a tune or melodic idea.

STEP 2

Because the left hand is so important rhythmically, work on getting it as even as you can. Also, try and find the natural feel of the beat (which is often again on '2' and '4'), and put an accent on it.

PART 3: JAZZ

THEORY

Jazz means different things to many people. While there are certain things you have to know, try and be guided by your gut feeling – it's meant to be a style of music that breaks free from rules and boundaries.

One of the most recognisable styles in jazz is 'swing'. Usually swing jazz has what is known as a 'walking' bassline – a constantly flowing series of notes that give the rhythm a solid foundation. Over the top of this walking bassline, other instruments – including the piano – are able to play more unusual rhythms and chords.

TIP

All the pieces in the section coming up have four beats in the bar. To help you get an idea of how fast they are, there is a figure given for tempo (meaning time). This will tell you how many beats per minute (or bpm) there are.

To make the music feel right, there are also some extra markings to help you out.

REPEATS: All the music between double bars with two dots on each stave is to be repeated. Because the double bars are at the start and end of each example, it means repeating the whole four-bar section.

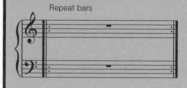

Repeat bars

TIED NOTES: Wherever you see a line joining up two notes, play one note of their combined length. In this example, a quarter note is joined to an eighth note, making a total length of one and a half beats.

IN PRACTICE

STEP 1

Like blues, jazz uses a mix of 'clashing' and 'normal' harmony. In the play-along section, you'll come across a few examples. We haven't got space here to go into jazz harmony in any detail, but if you want to learn more, how about getting a jazz chord book to help you? Also, listen to as much jazz as you can – all great players get ideas from other artists.

STEP 2

As you'll see in the 'In The Style Of...' section, there's a lot of what we call 'syncopation' in jazz. This is just a name given to chords or notes that are played off the beat. If you end up playing jazz, you'll often just have a chord chart to play from. This means you can choose, and feel, where to play chords, so it's a good idea to try out different places in the bar to play.

TEST

QUESTION 1
What kind of bassline does swing jazz usually have?

QUESTION 2
What is 'syncopation'?

QUESTION 3
What does 'bpm' stand for?

TOP 10 ARTISTS

TRACK 34 CD

ELTON JOHN

He may be one of this country's best known singer/songwriters, but Elton John's piano playing shouldn't be underestimated as a factor in his success. In fact, Elton trained as a classical pianist until he was 17, before trying his hand in the pop world. When he hit the big time, his distinctive piano style could be heard on huge hits like 'Your Song,' 'Daniel' and 'Rocket Man'. Elton could also rock out with the best of them, such as the classic 'Saturday Night's Alright For Fighting'.

Between 1972 and 1976, he wrote 16 straight Top 20 hits – a colossal achievement. No one could keep up that sort of output, and, after that period, Elton started to release albums on a regular, but less hectic, schedule. He continued to have huge hits through the '80s and '90s, including the massive 'Can You Feel The Love Tonight' from *The Lion King* soundtrack.

If there's one thing that marks out Elton John's piano playing, it's finding the right part for the song. You can always hear the piano very clearly, but it never gets in the way. That's the mark of a very skilful player.

STATISTICS

DATE OF BIRTH
25 March 1947

PLACE OF BIRTH
Pinner, Middlesex, England

INFLUENCES
Leon Russell, The Beach Boys, The Beatles, The Rolling Stones

FIRST HIT
'I've Been Loving You Too Long' – March 1968

HIGHEST CHART POSITION
'Crocodile Rock' – #1 – October 1972 (the first of many #1 hits)

INSTRUMENTS USED
Yamaha grand piano

LISTEN TO
'Your Song'
'Daniel'
'Candle In The Wind'
'Song For Guy'
'Crocodile Rock'

IN THE STYLE OF...

Elton John doesn't usually do anything radical with his piano parts, but they work extremely well. Look at these two examples below.

HOW TO PLAY LIKE ELTON JOHN

This is a medium-paced pop ballad in a typical Elton John style. The right-hand part mixes up straight major chords and arpeggios. Underneath, the left hand 'pedals' (stays on the same note over some of these chord changes) – classic Elton John.

To play the last right-hand chord, keep you thumb on the previous C note until your second and fourth fingers are over the D and B. Try not to move your hand around too much – get your fingers to do as much as you can.

A similar piece, but the left hand does a bit more to help along the rhythm here. Notice how the sustain pedal is used every two beats to stop the part from sounding messy.

The right hand plays quite a tuneful part. Try and bring it out as much as you can.

TRACK 35 & 36 CD

TRACK 37 & 38 CD

SUPERSTAR TIP!

One of the ways Elton keeps the rhythm interesting is to use syncopation. Syncopation happens here in the first and third bars of the second piece, where a note slightly anticipates – comes before – the third beat of the bar. The note is then tied over afterwards. Listen to the CD to help you out.

TRUE STORY!

Elton John wrote most of his songs with lyricist Bernie Taupin. Before they were famous, their publisher Dick James called them his 'little side project', not realising that one day they would be superstars!

CHRIS MARTIN

Chris Martin's piano playing has been a major factor in the success of his band Coldplay. Major hits like 'Trouble' and 'Clocks' strongly feature the piano. The band's sometimes understated style provides a good musical platform for simple, yet effective, piano parts.

The band's first album, *Parachutes*, was the starting point for a remarkable run of success. As well as 'Trouble', the tracks 'Yellow' and 'Shiver' were also Top 40 hits. Many thought it difficult to follow up with an equally strong second album, but *A Rush Of Blood To The Head* has been one of the most critically-acclaimed albums of the decade.

STATISTICS

DATE OF BIRTH
2 March 1977

PLACE OF BIRTH
Exeter, Devon

INFLUENCES
Bob Dylan, Neil Young, Tom Waits

FIRST HIT
'Shiver' – March 2000

HIGHEST CHART POSITION
'In My Place' – #2
– August 2002

LISTEN TO
'Trouble'
'Shiver'
'Clocks'

IN THE STYLE OF...

TRACK 39 & 40 CD

TRACK 41 & 42 CD

SUPERSTAR TIP!

When you use simple parts like these, dynamics and phrasing become even more important than usual. In this kind of four-in-the-bar time signature, put a slight accent on the second and fourth beats of the bar.

TRUE STORY!

While the band were recording their second album, Chris said that if it wasn't up to standard, they'd give up. Instead, it went multi-platinum, and helped the band to break into the American market!

Like all good singer/songwriters, Chris can make the piano fit around the song. When you listen to a track like 'Trouble', there's nothing really complicated going on – it's mostly a series of straight major and minor chords, played on the beat.

HOW TO PLAY LIKE CHRIS MARTIN

Coldplay's music often has a steady movement of major and minor chords. During an introduction (before the singing starts in the verse), there is often a melody played over the top of the chords, as in this first example.

This is a more typical verse part, to be played underneath a vocal line. Notice how the right hand chords are really very simple.

ALICIA KEYS

Alicia Keys performs her unique, piano-led style of r'n'b with gospel, blues and hip-hop influences. She took piano lessons from the age of seven, and continued them through her childhood, majoring at the Manhattan School of Performing Arts.

Having written her first song at 14, her talents were soon spotted, and she signed to a major record company at 18. A year later, her debut album, *Songs In The Key Of A Minor*, was released. It proved an instant hit, reaching #1 in the American Billboard charts. Hit singles included 'Fallin'', which reached #3 in the UK chart. Her follow-up album, *The Diary Of Alicia Keys*, which again mixes up her classical and r 'n' b influences, has been equally well received. It features her latest single 'If I Ain't Got You.'

STATISTICS

DATE OF BIRTH
25 January 1981

PLACE OF BIRTH
Manhattan, New York

INFLUENCES
Miles Davis, Nina Simone, Aretha Franklin

FIRST HIT/HIGHEST CHART POSITION
'Fallin'' – UK #3
– January 2002

LISTEN TO
'A Woman's Worth'
'Fallin''
'Girlfriend'
'If I Ain't Got You'

IN THE STYLE OF...

Alicia's style, like all the other featured artists here, comes from a huge mixture of influences. These include great classical composers, Beethoven and Chopin; soul and jazz artists, Aretha Franklin, Nina Simone and Stevie Wonder; and modern hip-hop/ r 'n' b rappers, Tupac Shakur and the Wu-Tang Clan.

HOW TO PLAY LIKE ALICIA KEYS

At the centre of most soul or r 'n' b tracks is a groove, normally laid down by the bass player. Sometimes, the piano player's left-hand part plays along with it, which is what happens here. Just get used to playing this round a few times first of all.

Alicia often puts quite jazzy chords like these over a groovy bassline. Sometimes, a whole track can be made up from one or two passages like this, just repeated round and round.

JOOLS HOLLAND

Though he is famous these days as a TV presenter, Jools Holland remains one of the UK's best-known piano players. A love of blues and boogie-woogie has always been at the centre of his playing style, though he shot to fame at a very young age as keyboardist for the pop group Squeeze. He was with the group through their most successful period, playing on hits such as 'Cool For Cats' and 'Up The Junction'. Jools then left to follow a solo career, his own albums more clearly showing off his individual style of playing.

He later rejoined Squeeze in 1985, and the band enjoyed some more success in the US. He was in demand as a session keyboard player too, and can be heard on many classic '80s tracks.

His work as a TV presenter took him from the '80s music show, *The Tube*, through to his current long-running series, *Later With Jools Holland*. As well as being one of the country's best known faces, he still plays and records music with his own big band. Lucky man!

STATISTICS

DATE OF BIRTH
24 January 1958

PLACE OF BIRTH
Deptford, London

INFLUENCES
Lee Dorsey, Jerry Lee Lewis, BB King

FIRST HIT
'Take Me I'm Yours' (with Squeeze) – January 1977

HIGHEST CHART POSITION
'Cool For Cats' – #2 – April 1979

LISTEN TO

WITH SQUEEZE:
'Cool For Cats'
'Up The Junction'
'Pulling Mussels'
'Hourglass'

AS A SOLO ARTIST:
'Steamhammer Boogie'
'Crazy Over You'

IN THE STYLE OF...

TRUE STORY!

Jools played a cameo part in the Spice Girls film *Spiceworld* (1997)!

Jools has a particularly energetic style of playing, which lends itself well to boogie-woogie. Although you can always hear this influence in his music, he's able to adapt to the musical situation he's in. Listen to his work with Squeeze to hear how he does this in a more pop-orientated band.

HOW TO PLAY LIKE JOOLS HOLLAND

This piece is a straightforward 12-bar boogie-woogie blues number. The left hand keeps the same pattern throughout, just moving up or down in pitch. Hear how a lot of the harmony is based around seventh chords, and how the occasional 'clash' of notes helps give the piece a distinctive bluesy sound.

Once you've got the left hand sorted for the first bar, you can use the same fingering for the rest of the piece.

This sign tells you to play the normal version of a note, not a flat or sharp

BEN FOLDS

Ben Folds first came on to the music scene with his band Ben Folds Five in 1994. His musical style is a mixture of pop, rock and show-style melodies, punched along by his very energetic piano playing. Known for his off-the-wall live performances, Ben sometimes breaks out of a song and will just start making something up!

There were only actually three people in Ben Folds Five – Ben, bass player Robert Sledge and drummer Darren Jesse. That they were able to produce such an exciting, rocky sound without a guitar gives you an idea of Ben's powerful playing. Though his vocal melodies are very catchy, a lot of his songs are best known for their piano solos.

After he left the band to follow a solo career in 2000, Ben's piano playing and personality continued to win him new fans the world over. Amazingly, Ben now plays all the instruments on his albums – piano, guitar and drums!

STATISTICS

DATE OF BIRTH
12 September 1966

PLACE OF BIRTH
Winston-Salem, North Carolina, USA

INFLUENCES
Elton John, Cole Porter, The Clash

FIRST HIT
'Underground'
– September 1996

HIGHEST CHART POSITION
'Brick' – UK #26
– April 1998

FAVOURITE PIANO
Baldwin

LISTEN TO
'Army'
'Kate'
'One Angry Dwarf'
'Philosophy'
'Narcolepsy'

IN THE STYLE OF...

Ben Folds doesn't believe in only doing things the 'correct' way – it's not unusual to see him playing the piano with his elbows, or mashing notes together! If you catch him at a live concert, you're never quite sure what's going to happen.

HOW TO PLAY LIKE BEN FOLDS

This is typical of Ben's more straightforward pieces. Having said that, it needs to be played in the right way, with accents on the second and fourth beats, to groove along properly. There are markings above the notes to help you remember.

TRACKS 49 & 50

Ben Folds uses a lot of arpeggiated ideas like this one for his faster lines. Although the left hand moves up and down an octave, notice that it stays on a C.

TRACKS 51 & 52

SUPERSTAR TIP!

Ben sees the piano as a rock 'n' roll instrument, just like a guitar, and plays it like one, too! Though he sometimes breaks the 'rules', he's a very exciting player to listen to.

TRUE STORY!

The author Nick Hornby was so impressed with Ben's song 'Smoke' that he called it 'perfect'!

NINA SIMONE

Nina was a gifted child who started playing piano in her mother's church at the age of four. She was so small, her feet weren't able to reach the pedals!

Nina trained in New York to become a classical pianist, but started playing in clubs and bars to support her family. This was a tough introduction to working life.

She was soon making a name for herself by composing, singing and arranging her recordings. Her style combined a lot of different influences – jazz, gospel, blues and classical. Nina was a very expressive live performer, and a master of making the music really mean something.

Sadly, Nina experienced a lot of racism during her career, both personally and as part of the wider issues in '60s America. She channelled a lot of her anger into music, using songs to express her feelings about civil rights.

She continued to tour and record music right through to her death in 2003, and enjoyed a big surge in popularity in the '80s, with a re-release of one of her previous hits, 'My Baby Just Cares For Me'. Nina was a very charismatic artist and a true legend.

STATISTICS

DATE OF BIRTH
21 February 1933

PLACE OF BIRTH
Tyron, North Carolina, USA

INFLUENCES
JS Bach, Maria Callas, Frank Sinatra

FIRST HIT /HIGHEST CHART POSITION
'Ain't Got No – I Got Life/ Do What You Gotta Do' – #2 – December 1968

LISTEN TO

'Plain Gold Ring'
'Little Girl Blue'
'Feeling Good'
'My Baby Just Cares For Me'
'I Loves You, Porgy'

IN THE STYLE OF...

Through her mixture of classical and jazz styles, Nina Simone established a unique style that won her a huge fan base. You can learn a lot about performing and feel by listening to her recordings.

HOW TO PLAY LIKE NINA SIMONE

This first piece uses a new type of notation, called a triplet. There are three eighth notes making up a beat, instead of two. When you 'vamp' like this with two hands, using triplets can help give a more swing-like, groovy feel. Don't forget to listen to the CD to help you out.

This next piece is a complete contrast, in the style of one of Nina's emotional ballads. Taking maximum notice of the dynamic markings will help you to get it sounding good.

This sign means 'pause', so just hold on the note a couple of beats longer

SUPERSTAR TIP!

To get a touch like Nina's, which is very even and sensitive, make sure you reach the bottom of each note, like I told you in the scales lesson. This helps you to play quiet passages with maximum control.

TRUE STORY!

Nina changed her name from Eunice Waymon when she started to play professionally in clubs and bars. 'Nina' means 'Little One' and 'Simone' came from the name of a French actress called Simone Signoret.

TRACKS 53 & 54

TRACKS 55 & 56

BILLY JOEL

A product of a tough upbringing in New York's Bronx, Billy was another player who started off with a classical training; however, he started playing in nightclubs as a teenager to help his family's income.

When he saw The Beatles during their 1964 US tour, he decided to make rock 'n' roll his main direction in life. He joined a band – The Echoes – and started as a session player at the tender age of 16. It wasn't exactly overnight success for Billy, though. After a few projects bombed, he took some time out from music. After a while he realised his dream was to have success as a singer/songwriter.

Billy was able to combine the strong melodies of Broadway-like stage shows and bands like The Beatles. Again, it took a while for him to find success, but, after the triumph of huge albums like *Piano Man* and *The Stranger*, he became a megastar. He enjoyed continued popularity through the '80s and '90s with later albums, such as *An Innocent Man* and *Storm Front*. Returning to his classical roots, Billy released an album of solo piano compositions, *Fantasies And Delusions*, in 2001.

STATISTICS

DATE OF BIRTH
9 May 1949

PLACE OF BIRTH
Bronx, New York, USA

INFLUENCES
JS Bach, Beethoven, Ray Charles, Otis Redding

FIRST HIT
'Just The Way You Are' – January 1978

HIGHEST CHART POSITION
'Uptown Girl' – #1 – October 1983

LISTEN TO
'Piano Man'
'Just The Way You Are'
'Uptown Girl'
'Honesty'
'An Innocent Man'

IN THE STYLE OF...

As one of the biggest-selling artists of all time, Billy Joel has every right to feel proud of his achievements. However, when he wrote his album for solo piano, *Fantasies And Delusions*, he declined to play on the recording, instead handing over the task to Richard Joo, a young virtuoso pianist. 'I'm not as good a pianist as people think I am,' he said, modestly, '…but I'm OK for rock 'n' roll!'

HOW TO PLAY LIKE BILLY JOEL

Billy often uses a mixture of simple and more complex chords in his music. This first piece, a classic pop piano ballad, is a good example. Notice how he uses syncopation between the left and right hands to help along the rhythm.

This next example is a more up-tempo, pop-style track.

TORI AMOS

The daughter of a church minister, Tori was another child prodigy who studied at a classical conservatory. However, she went her own way when the school insisted on too strict a classical education. Playing in bars and clubs from the age of 16, she later joined various bands before striking out on her own solo career.

Gaining recognition for her very personal style of songwriting and exceptional piano playing, her breakthrough came with the album, *Little Earthquakes*, which was released in 1991. A follow-up album, *Under The Pink*, was equally successful, featuring hits such as 'Cornflake Girl' and 'Pretty Good Year'.

Her skill at arranging could be heard in her third album, *Boys For Pele*, which featured orchestras and choirs. On the opposite end of the scale, her song 'Professional Widow' was remixed by dance artist Armand Van Helden and became a massive hit. This opened up her music to a wider audience than she had ever had before.

Her most recent albums, *Songs From The Choirgirl Hotel*, *To Venus And Back*, *Strange Little Girls* and *Tales Of A Librarian*, show her making the kind of music she wants to. She remains a unique talent with a very distinctive playing style.

STATISTICS

DATE OF BIRTH
22 August 1963

PLACE OF BIRTH
Newton, North Carolina, USA

INFLUENCES
John Lennon, The Doors, Joni Mitchell

FIRST HIT
'Winter' – November 1992

HIGHEST CHART POSITION
'Professional Widow' (remix) – UK #1 – January 1997

LISTEN TO
'Winter'
'Crucify'
'Cornflake Girl'
'Spark'

IN THE STYLE OF...

Tori's style of playing is quite different to most artists in this book. She doesn't use a lot of straight major or minor chords, instead making up her own style of harmony. She often leaves out the third (harmony) note in chords, giving a distinctive, bare sound. You can hear this in the first example.

HOW TO PLAY LIKE TORI AMOS

In this first example, we use the eighth-note triplet again. If you're not sure how to read it, listen to the CD to guide you. You can hold down the pedal for a whole bar at a time, but be careful to re-use it for the next bar. Don't let it bleed over.

132 bpm

TRACKS 61 & 62

This is a more subdued, sensitive piece, but again with the same type of bare-sounding chords. Sometimes less is more!

87 bpm

TRACKS 63 & 64

SUPERSTAR TIP!

Tori Amos gets her unique sound by taking normal harmony and then changing it. When you're trying to make up something yourself, don't be afraid to experiment and find new chords of your own.

TRUE STORY!

Early on in her career, Tori's musical style wasn't thought to be very American radio-friendly, so she was based in the UK for a while, and still has a house here!

JAMIE CULLUM

Jamie got into music at an early age, and by the time he was eight years old had taken up guitar and the piano. Realising that he wanted some time out to concentrate on his music, Jamie took a year off before he went to university. He spent his time travelling, listening to music and eventually playing in pubs and cafés in Paris.

While he was at university, he continued to develop his jazz playing and was gigging in and around the London area. He produced CDs of his own, which he sold at gigs, and a copy found its way to Alan Bates, a well-known producer.

More recording followed and Jamie began to get radio airplay. Major record labels became interested, and before long Jamie was signed up to make several albums. Soon, he was everywhere, from the *Parkinson* TV show to the Queens' birthday party at Buckingham Palace. Not bad for a 24-year-old…

STATISTICS

DATE OF BIRTH
1980

PLACE OF BIRTH
Wiltshire, UK

INFLUENCES
Frank Sinatra, Nirvana, Jeff Buckley

FIRST HIT/HIGHEST CHART POSITION
'These Are The Days/Frontin' – #12 – March 2004

LISTEN TO

'I Could Have Danced All Night'
'Wind Cries Mary'
'Twentysomething'

IN THE STYLE OF...

Jamie combines a mixture of new and old. On the one hand, he is clearly influenced by well-known jazz artists such as Frank Sinatra, Thelonius Monk, and Ella Fitzgerald. On the other, his more modern love of rock music can be heard on his cover of the Jimi Hendrix track, 'Wind Cries Mary'.

HOW TO PLAY LIKE JAMIE CULLUM

This left hand groove uses a heavy blues influence, combined with more eighth-note triplets. These help give a definite 'swing' feel.

145 bpm

Jazz music often features what are called 'stops', when the whole band plays punchy, stabbing chords. Sometimes, a drummer will solo over the gaps, as he does here.

SUPERSTAR TIP!

Jamie uses a lot of major seventh and minor seventh chords, which are basically straight majors and minors with added seventh intervals. Why don't you get a chord book and start looking at some of these?

TRUE STORY!

Jamie didn't think of having a professional music career until he ran out of tunes while performing at his local pub. He then played and sung a jazz standard 'Do You Know What It Means To Miss New Orleans?' From the audience reaction, he realised he might have a future in the business...

TRACKS 65 & 66

TRACKS 67 & 68

DIANA KRALL

Over the last decade, Diana Krall has become one of the world's most popular jazz artists. Often performing with just a small group of musicians, she still manages to sell out large concert halls the world over. Her first recording, *Stepping Out*, was released in 1993, and since then she has had an incredibly successful career. She has been nominated for a Grammy award and many of her albums have gone multi-platinum – a real achievement for a jazz artist.

Born near Vancouver, Canada, Diana took inspiration from her father, who was himself an accomplished player. Her interest was sparked from a young age, and, as a teenager, she was awarded a place at the Berklee College of Music in Boston, USA, which is one of the world's most famous music conservatories.

Though best known for playing jazz standards, Diana has more recently released some of her own, original material, most recently this year with the album *The Girl In The Other Room*.

STATISTICS

DATE OF BIRTH
16 November 1964

PLACE OF BIRTH
Nanaimo, British Columbia, Canada

INFLUENCES
Dinah Washington, Roberta Flack, Fats Waller, Frank Sinatra

FIRST RECORDING
Stepping Out
– September 1993

HIGHEST CHART POSITION
When I Look in Your Eyes
– US Billboard chart #1
– June 1999

LISTEN TO
Live In Paris
When I Look In Your Eyes
Only Trust Your Heart

IN THE STYLE OF...

As a lover of jazz standards, Diana Krall plays a lot of swing-type rhythms. This often has a walking bassline with the right hand playing a lot of syncopated rhythms over the top. Syncopation means accenting notes and chords that are off the beat.

HOW TO PLAY LIKE DIANA KRALL

We're going to play through a chord progression first of all, and then, in the next piece, have a go at a solo part. In the first piece, the right hand plays some syncopated chords over the bassline. Listen to the CD to help you here. Before trying to play it up to speed, just get comfortable with the order each hand plays in.

The CD will play the backing for this one, as you use the right hand to play a solo part. It uses eighth note triplets again to help give that swing feel. Don't be afraid of this part – it's all pretty much based around C major, apart from the last bit of the second bar. To make it sound good, listen to how the example on the CD accents certain notes. This helps give it a good feel.

155 bpm

FINAL ADVICE FROM KEYS

Reading about famous artists, you can see that success doesn't always happen overnight. Sometimes things just take a bit of time. If you stick at it, though, eventually you stand a good chance of getting somewhere.

So, don't worry if you have times when you feel you're not making progress in your playing. Everyone has times like that. But you sure won't get anywhere if you give up. Even when things don't seem to be going your way, by carrying on, you're still moving forward. Improvements often come in sudden leaps.

As you move on through your musical life, you're going to meet and see other piano players. Don't be discouraged if you think you're not as good as someone else. Music is not just about how fast you can play or how flashy you sound. You will always be able to do something they can't – because music is about expressing your personality. Enjoy!

APPENDIX: MINOR SCALES

Pure A minor scale, right hand

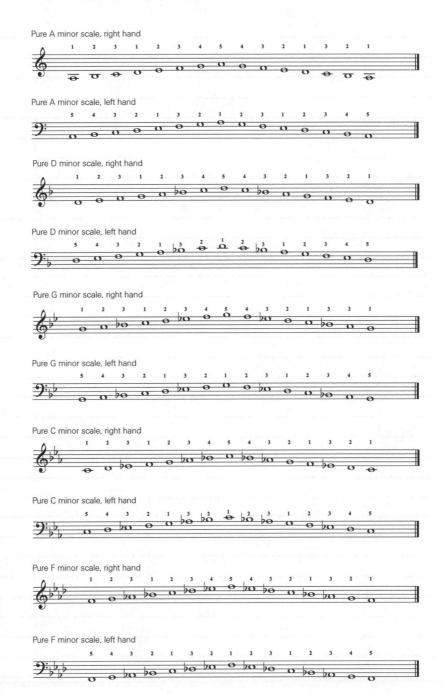

Pure A minor scale, left hand

Pure D minor scale, right hand

Pure D minor scale, left hand

Pure G minor scale, right hand

Pure G minor scale, left hand

Pure C minor scale, right hand

Pure C minor scale, left hand

Pure F minor scale, right hand

Pure F minor scale, left hand

NOTES

GLOSSARY

12-BAR BLUES
An arrangement of three chords over a set 12-bar length.

ARPEGGIO
The notes of a chord played separately in succession.

BAR
The way a number of beats (in this book, four) is felt and divided in a piece of music.

BARLINE
The point in the music dividing each group of beats.

CHORD
A selection of at least three notes played at the same time.

COMMON TIME
Another way of describing four beats in the bar.

EIGHTH NOTE
A note that lasts for half a beat in common time.

FLAT
When a flat sign (♭) is placed before a note, it tells you to lower it by a semitone

HALF NOTE
A note that lasts for two beats in common time.

INTERVAL
The distance between two notes.

INVERSION
A chord that uses the same notes as a root position major or minor, but with the notes arranged in a different order.

KEY SIGNATURE
How many sharps or flats there are in a key.

LEGATO
Italian musical term meaning 'smoothly'.

MAJOR
An arrangement of notes within a scale or a chord that has a sharpened third step.

MINOR
An arrangement of notes within a scale or a chord that has a flattened third step.

MIDDLE C
The C note found in the middle of the keyboard, between the two pedals.

OCTAVE
Two notes with the same key letter name that are eight scale-based steps apart.

QUARTER NOTE
A note length that lasts for a beat in common time.

ROOT POSITION
Describes the position of a chord when its key note is at the bottom.

SEMITONE
The distance (or interval) between two adjacent notes on the keyboard.

SHARP
When you see a sharp sign (♯) placed before a note it tells you to raise it by a semitone.

SIXTEENTH NOTE
A note that lasts for quarter of a beat in common time.

SYNCOPATION
Describes music that is accented off the beat.

TIME SIGNATURE
A description of the amount of beats in each bar, and the length of each beat.

TONE
An interval of two semitones.

ANSWERS TO TEST QUESTIONS

LESSON 1
1. Grand and upright.
2. Middle C.
3. The sustain pedal.

LESSON 2
1. Smoothly.
2. C major.

LESSON 3
1. The first, third and fifth notes.
2. One sharp (F sharp).
3. Accidentals.

LESSON 4
1. Four beats.
2. One beat.
3. A whole note.

LESSON 5
Audio test using the CD.

LESSON 6
1. Root position.
2. Major chord.
3. Blues.

LESSON 7
Have a break!

LESSON 8
1. Either:
• To make the change from one chord to another as smooth as possible.
• To keep sounding part of a chord while you play other notes.
2. The left hand helps keep the rhythm flowing.

LESSON 9
1. f
2. p
3. diminuendo (dim)
4. crescendo (cresc)

LESSON 10
1. Walking bassline.
2. Music that is accented off the beat.
3. Beats per minute.